How to Make Money with a Chatbot

By

Dr Chris Egbu

Author

Of

- How to Make Money Online

- How to Gain Clients

- 20 Easy Steps to Be More Productive,

- Entrepreneurial Finance-How To Raise Capital to Start Your Business

&

- Newways of Employee Empowerment

Also available on Amazon

How to Make Money with a Chatbot

How to Make Money with a Chatbot

Table of Contents

Chapter 3. Monetizing Your Chatbot

A. Generating revenue through lead generation and customer acquisition

B. Implementing e-commerce features and integrating payment gateways

C. Leveraging chatbot advertising and sponsorship opportunities

D. Offering premium services or subscriptions through the chatbot

E. Exploring partnerships and affiliate marketing options

Chapter 4. Marketing and Promoting Your Chatbot

A. Creating a compelling chatbot marketing strategy

B. Leveraging social media and content marketing to promote your chatbot

C. Utilizing email marketing and targeted campaigns

D. Optimizing your chatbot for search engines and discoverability

E. Measuring and analyzing the performance of your marketing efforts

Chapter 5. Ensuring Compliance and Security

A. Understanding legal and privacy considerations for chatbots

B. Complying with data protection regulations and securing user information

C. Implementing safeguards against malicious activities and fraud

D. Maintaining ethical standards in chatbot interactions

Chapter 6. Chatbot Success Stories

A. Case studies of businesses that have successfully monetized chatbots

B. Lessons learned and key takeaways from their experiences

C. Insights into their strategies and implementation approaches

Chapter 7. Future Trends and Opportunities

A. Emerging technologies and innovations in the chatbot space

B. Predictions for the future of chatbot monetization

C. Opportunities for business growth and expansion through chatbots

Conclusion

A. Recap of key concepts and strategies discussed

B. Final words of encouragement and inspiration

C. Call to action to start monetizing chatbots and make money

X. Appendix

A. Resources for chatbot development platforms and tools

B. Glossary of key terms and acronyms

C. Frequently asked questions (FAQs) about chatbot monetization

How to Make Money with a Chatbot

Introduction

A. The rise of chatbots in business

B. Overview of the book's purpose and structure

A. The Rise of Chatbots in Business

In recent years, chatbots have emerged as powerful tools that are revolutionizing the way businesses interact with their customers. From customer support and sales to marketing and lead generation, chatbots have proven to be versatile and efficient in streamlining business processes and enhancing user experiences. The rise of artificial intelligence (AI) and natural language processing (NLP) technologies has further fueled the growth of chatbots, enabling them to understand and respond to human queries with remarkable accuracy.

B. Overview of the Book's Purpose and Structure

The purpose of this book is to provide a comprehensive guide on how to leverage chatbots to make money in the business world. Whether you are a small business owner, a marketer, or an entrepreneur looking to tap into the potential of chatbots, this book will equip you with the knowledge and strategies needed to monetize your chatbot effectively.

The book is structured to take you through a step-by-step journey, starting with the fundamentals of chatbots and gradually diving into the intricacies of building, monetizing, marketing, and securing your chatbot. Each chapter is designed to provide practical insights, tips, and real-world examples that will help you navigate the complexities of chatbot monetization.

By the end of this book, you will have a thorough understanding of the opportunities chatbots present for generating revenue, as well as the tools and techniques required to maximize their potential. Whether you are considering integrating a chatbot into your existing business or starting a new venture centred around chatbot services, this book will serve as your comprehensive guide to making money with chatbots.

Now, let's embark on this exciting journey together and explore the world of chatbot monetization.

Chapter 1. Understanding Chatbots

A. Definition and types of chatbots

B. Benefits and potential of chatbots for business

C. Common use cases for chatbots

A. Definition and Types of Chatbots

Before delving into the monetization aspects, it's essential to have a clear understanding of what chatbots are and the different types available. A chatbot, also known as a conversational agent, is a computer program designed to simulate human conversation through text or voice interactions. These interactions can take place on websites, messaging apps, social media platforms, or standalone chatbot applications.

There are various types of chatbots, each with its own capabilities and functionalities. Some common types include:

Rule-Based Chatbots: Rule-based chatbots operate on predefined rules and scripts. They follow a decision-tree structure and provide pre-determined responses based on specific keywords or patterns in user input.

AI-Powered Chatbots: AI-powered chatbots leverage artificial intelligence and machine learning algorithms to interpret and respond to user queries. They can understand natural language and adapt their responses based on context and user behaviour.

Virtual Assistants: Virtual assistants, such as Apple's Siri, Amazon's Alexa, or Google Assistant, are advanced chatbots that combine AI, NLP, and voice recognition technologies. They can perform tasks like answering questions, setting reminders, and controlling smart devices.

B. Benefits and Potential of Chatbots for Business

Chatbots offer a range of benefits and have the potential to transform various aspects of business operations. Some key advantages include:

Enhanced Customer Service: Chatbots provide instant and personalized assistance to customers, improving response times and overall customer satisfaction. They can handle common queries, provide product recommendations, and offer 24/7 support.

Increased Efficiency and Scalability: Chatbots can handle multiple conversations simultaneously, eliminating the need for customers to wait for human assistance. This scalability improves efficiency, reduces costs, and allows businesses to handle high volumes of inquiries.

Lead Generation and Qualification: Chatbots can engage with website visitors or social media users, capturing leads and qualifying them based on specific criteria. This automated lead-generation process helps businesses identify potential customers and nurture them through the sales funnel.

Sales and E-commerce: Chatbots can facilitate seamless sales transactions by guiding customers through the purchasing process, answering product-related questions, and offering personalized recommendations. They can also integrate with e-commerce platforms, enabling customers to make purchases directly within the chatbot interface.

C. Common Use Cases for Chatbots

Chatbots find applications across various industries and business functions. Some common use cases include:

Customer Support: Chatbots can handle customer inquiries, provide product information, troubleshoot issues, and escalate complex problems to human agents when necessary.

Marketing and Lead Generation: Chatbots can engage with website visitors, collect contact information, and qualify leads based on predefined criteria. They can also deliver targeted marketing messages and promotions.

E-commerce and Sales: Chatbots can assist customers in finding products, making purchase recommendations, and facilitating seamless transactions. They can also provide post-sales support and order-tracking information.

Appointment Scheduling: Chatbots can automate the scheduling process by allowing users to book appointments, check availability, and receive reminders, reducing administrative burdens.

Understanding the definition, types, benefits, and common use cases of chatbots sets the foundation for effectively harnessing their potential for monetization.

Chapter 2. Building a Successful Chatbot

A. Identifying your business goals and target audience

B. Choosing the right chatbot platform or framework

C. Designing an intuitive and user-friendly chatbot interface

D. Integrating AI and natural language processing capabilities

E. Testing and refining your chatbot for optimal performance

A. Identifying Your Business Goals and Target Audience

Before diving into chatbot development, it's crucial to identify your business goals and understand your target audience. Clearly define the purpose of your chatbot, whether it is to provide customer support, generate leads, facilitate sales, or offer personalized recommendations. By aligning your chatbot's functionalities with your business goals, you can create a more effective and focused solution.

Additionally, understanding your target audience is essential for crafting the right user experience. Consider their preferences, needs, and pain points to design a chatbot that resonates with them and addresses their specific requirements.

B. Choosing the Right Chatbot Platform or Framework

Selecting the appropriate chatbot platform or framework is a critical step in building a successful chatbot. There are numerous options available, each with its own features, capabilities, and integration possibilities. Some popular choices include:

Prebuilt Chatbot Platforms: These platforms provide ready-to-use chatbot templates and frameworks, allowing you to quickly set up a chatbot without extensive coding. Examples include Dialogflow, IBM Watson Assistant, and Amazon Lex.

Custom Development: If you require more flexibility and control over your chatbot's functionalities, custom development using programming languages and frameworks like Python, Node.js, or Rasa can be a suitable option.

Evaluate the features, scalability, ease of integration, and pricing options of different platforms to find the one that best aligns with your requirements.

C. Designing an Intuitive and User-Friendly Chatbot Interface

The design of your chatbot interface plays a crucial role in user engagement and satisfaction. Aim for an intuitive and user-friendly interface that guides users through the conversation flow seamlessly. Consider the following design principles:

Conversational Flow: Design a logical flow that allows users to easily navigate through different stages of the conversation. Use clear and concise language to guide users and ensure they understand the available options.

Visual Elements: Incorporate visual elements such as buttons, cards, and quick replies to provide users with clear response options and make the interaction more visually appealing.

Personalization: Tailor the chatbot's responses to the user's context and preferences whenever possible. Personalization can enhance the user experience and make the chatbot feel more relevant and helpful.

D. Integrating AI and Natural Language Processing Capabilities

Integrating AI and natural language processing (NLP) capabilities into your chatbot can significantly enhance its effectiveness. AI-powered chatbots can understand and respond to user queries more intelligently, leading to more natural and engaging conversations. Consider the following techniques:

Natural Language Understanding (NLU): Implement NLU techniques to extract the intent and entities from user messages. This allows your chatbot to understand user requests accurately and provide relevant responses.

Machine Learning: Train your chatbot using machine learning algorithms to improve its understanding of user input over time. This can help your chatbot adapt to various user scenarios and continuously improve its performance.

Sentiment Analysis: Incorporate sentiment analysis capabilities to understand user emotions and respond accordingly. This can enable your chatbot to provide empathetic and appropriate responses, enhancing the user experience.

E. Testing and Refining Your Chatbot for Optimal Performance

Testing and refining your chatbot are essential steps in ensuring its optimal performance. Conduct thorough testing to identify and resolve any issues or bugs. Consider the following testing techniques:

Functional Testing: Test your chatbot's functionalities to ensure it responds accurately to user inputs and covers all use cases.

User Testing: Conduct user testing sessions with individuals from your target audience to gather feedback and identify areas for improvement. This can help you refine the user experience and make necessary adjustments.

Continuous Improvement: Monitor user interactions and analyze data to identify patterns, common issues, and areas where the chatbot can be further optimized. Continuously refine and update your chatbot based on user feedback and evolving business needs.

By following these steps, you can build a successful chatbot that aligns with your business goals, provides a seamless user experience, and incorporates AI capabilities for intelligent interactions.

Chapter 3. Monetizing Your Chatbot

A. Generating revenue through lead generation and customer acquisition

B. Implementing e-commerce features and integrating payment gateways

C. Leveraging chatbot advertising and sponsorship opportunities

D. Offering premium services or subscriptions through the chatbot

E. Exploring partnerships and affiliate marketing options

A. Generating Revenue Through Lead Generation and Customer Acquisition

One way to monetize your chatbot is by leveraging it as a tool for lead generation and customer acquisition. By engaging with users and collecting their contact information, you can build a valuable database of potential customers. You can then nurture these leads through targeted marketing campaigns, email newsletters, or personalized offers, ultimately converting them into paying customers.

B. Implementing E-commerce Features and Integrating Payment Gateways

Integrating e-commerce features into your chatbot opens up opportunities for direct sales and revenue generation. Enable users to browse products, access product information, and make purchases seamlessly within the chatbot interface. Integrate secure payment gateways to facilitate transactions and provide a smooth and secure purchasing experience for your customers.

C. Leveraging Chatbot Advertising and Sponsorship Opportunities

Chatbots offer unique advertising and sponsorship opportunities. You can monetize your chatbot by partnering with other businesses and displaying their ads or sponsored content within the chatbot interface. This can be done through banner ads, sponsored messages, or native advertising. Ensure that the ads are relevant to your audience and align with your chatbot's purpose to maintain a positive user experience.

D. Offering Premium Services or Subscriptions Through the Chatbot

Consider offering premium services or subscription-based features through your chatbot. Identify valuable functionalities or exclusive content that users would be willing to pay for. This could include access to advanced features, personalized recommendations, premium support, or exclusive content. Implement a subscription model or offer one-time purchases to monetize these premium offerings.

E. Exploring Partnerships and Affiliate Marketing Options

Explore partnerships and affiliate marketing opportunities to monetize your chatbot. Collaborate with relevant brands or businesses and promote their products or services within your chatbot. This can be done through affiliate links, where you earn a commission for every referral or sale generated through your chatbot. Ensure that the partnerships align with your chatbot's audience and maintain transparency with your users about any affiliate relationships.

It's important to strike a balance between monetization and user experience. Avoid overwhelming users with excessive ads or intrusive monetization strategies, as this can lead to a negative user experience and potentially drive users away. Focus on providing value to your users and offering monetization options that enhance their overall experience with the chatbot.

F. Providing Sponsored Content and Native Advertising

Another way to monetize your chatbot is by offering sponsored content and native advertising. Collaborate with brands or businesses to create custom content that aligns with your chatbot's purpose and resonates with your target audience. This could include sponsored articles, product recommendations, or interactive experiences. Ensure that the sponsored content is clearly labelled as such to maintain transparency with your users.

G. Offering Data Insights and Analytics

If your chatbot collects and analyzes user data, you can monetize this information by providing data insights and analytics to businesses. Aggregate and anonymize the data to ensure privacy and compliance with regulations. Businesses can use these insights to gain valuable consumer behaviour information, market trends, or customer preferences, which can inform their decision-making and marketing strategies.

H. Providing Chatbot-as-a-Service (CaaS)

Consider offering your chatbot as a service to other businesses. Develop a scalable and customizable chatbot solution that can be white-labeled and offered to companies in various industries. This can be particularly appealing to businesses that want to incorporate chatbot functionality into their operations but lack the resources or expertise to develop a chatbot from scratch.

I. Licensing or Selling Your Chatbot Technology

If you have developed a highly advanced and specialized chatbot technology, you may explore licensing or selling it to other businesses or organizations. This can be done by offering your chatbot technology as a software package, API, or platform that others can integrate into their own products or services. Ensure that you have appropriate intellectual property protection in place before pursuing this monetization avenue.

J. Offering Consultation and Customization Services

Leverage your expertise in chatbot development and implementation by offering consultation and customization services. Businesses may require assistance in designing and building chatbots tailored to their specific needs. Provide guidance, training, and support to help businesses create effective chatbot solutions. This can be offered as a one-time service or as an ongoing partnership.

As with any monetization strategy, it's important to consider the value proposition for your users and ensure that the monetization methods align with your chatbot's purpose and target audience. Strive to strike a balance between generating revenue and delivering a positive user experience.

Regularly assess and adapt your monetization strategies based on user feedback, market trends, and the evolving needs of your target audience. By continuously refining and optimizing your monetization approach, you can maximize the revenue potential of your chatbot while maintaining user satisfaction and loyalty.

Remember to regularly analyze and track the performance of your monetization strategies. Monitor key metrics such as conversion rates, average revenue per user, and customer feedback to optimize your monetization efforts over time.

By implementing these monetization strategies, you can generate revenue from your chatbot while providing value to your users and enhancing their overall experience.

Chapter 4. Marketing and Promoting Your Chatbot

A. Creating a compelling chatbot marketing strategy

B. Leveraging social media and content marketing to promote your chatbot

C. Utilizing email marketing and targeted campaigns

D. Optimizing your chatbot for search engines and discoverability

E. Measuring and analyzing the performance of your marketing efforts

A. Creating a Compelling Chatbot Marketing Strategy

Develop a comprehensive chatbot marketing strategy to effectively promote your chatbot and reach your target audience. Define your unique selling points and value proposition, and identify the channels and tactics that will resonate with your audience. Set clear goals and establish key performance indicators (KPIs) to measure the success of your marketing efforts.

B. Leveraging Social Media and Content Marketing to Promote Your Chatbot

Utilize social media platforms to create awareness and generate interest in your chatbot. Share engaging and informative content related to your chatbot's functionalities, benefits, and use cases. Leverage visual content, such as videos and infographics, to make your messaging more compelling. Engage with your audience by responding to comments, addressing queries, and fostering discussions.

Additionally, implement content marketing strategies to attract and educate your target audience. Create blog posts, articles, or whitepapers that highlight the value of your chatbot and its impact on solving specific pain points. Optimize your content with relevant keywords to improve search engine visibility.

C. Utilizing Email Marketing and Targeted Campaigns

Email marketing can be an effective tool for promoting your chatbot. Build an email list of interested users and regularly send updates, newsletters, or exclusive content related to your chatbot. Tailor your messages to specific segments of your audience based on their interests, behaviours, or engagement levels to increase relevance and engagement.

Moreover, launch targeted marketing campaigns to reach potential users who may benefit from your chatbot. Utilize segmentation and personalization techniques to deliver tailored messages that address their specific pain points and showcase how your chatbot can provide solutions.

D. Optimizing Your Chatbot for Search Engines and Discoverability

To improve the discoverability of your chatbot, optimize it for search engines. Ensure that your chatbot's website or landing page has relevant keywords, meta tags, and descriptive content that accurately represents its functionalities and benefits. Consider implementing search engine optimization (SEO) best practices to increase organic visibility and attract users who are actively searching for chatbot solutions.

Additionally, leverage app stores or chatbot directories by optimizing your chatbot's listing with relevant keywords, engaging descriptions, and high-quality visuals. Encourage satisfied users to leave positive reviews and ratings, as these can boost your chatbot's credibility and visibility.

E. Measuring and Analyzing the Performance of Your Marketing Efforts

Regularly measure and analyze the performance of your marketing efforts to understand what's working and what needs improvement. Track key metrics such as website traffic, conversion rates, engagement levels, and user feedback. Utilize analytics tools to gain insights into user behavior, demographics, and acquisition sources.

Based on these insights, refine your marketing strategies and tactics. Experiment with A/B testing to optimize your messaging, visuals, and calls-to-action. Continuously adapt your marketing efforts to align with the evolving needs and preferences of your target audience.

By implementing a well-rounded marketing strategy, leveraging social media and content marketing, utilizing email campaigns, optimizing for search engines, and measuring performance, you can effectively promote your chatbot and maximize its reach and impact among your target audience.

Chapter 5. Ensuring Compliance and Security

A. Understanding legal and privacy considerations for chatbots

B. Complying with data protection regulations and securing user information

C. Implementing safeguards against malicious activities and fraud

D. Maintaining ethical standards in chatbot interactions

A. Understanding Legal and Privacy Considerations for Chatbots

When developing and deploying a chatbot, it is crucial to understand and comply with relevant legal and privacy considerations. Familiarize yourself with laws and regulations pertaining to data protection, consumer rights, and privacy in the jurisdictions where your chatbot operates. Ensure that your chatbot's activities align with these requirements to protect user privacy and avoid legal issues.

B. Complying with Data Protection Regulations and Securing User Information

Data protection is of utmost importance when operating a chatbot. Adhere to data protection regulations such as the General Data Protection Regulation (GDPR) or other applicable laws in your region. Implement measures to securely collect, store, and handle user information. This includes obtaining appropriate consent for data collection, providing transparency about data usage, and ensuring the confidentiality and integrity of user data.

Apply industry-standard security practices to protect user information from unauthorized access, breaches, or misuse. Encrypt sensitive data, regularly update software and security patches, and employ secure protocols for data transmission. Conduct regular security audits and assessments to identify and address vulnerabilities.

C. Implementing Safeguards Against Malicious Activities and Fraud

Chatbots can be vulnerable to malicious activities and fraud attempts. Implement safeguards to protect your chatbot and its users. Use authentication mechanisms to verify user identities and prevent unauthorized access. Employ measures to detect and mitigate common threats such as phishing, spam, or malware attacks. Monitor chatbot interactions for suspicious behavior and employ machine learning algorithms or natural language processing techniques to identify and mitigate potential risks.

D. Maintaining Ethical Standards in Chatbot Interactions

Ethics should be a critical consideration in chatbot development and operation. Ensure that your chatbot adheres to ethical standards and respects user rights.

Avoid engaging in deceptive practices, misrepresentation, or manipulation of users. Clearly disclose the chatbot's nature and limitations to users to avoid confusion. Provide users with options to opt-out or unsubscribe from communications if desired. Regularly monitor and review chatbot interactions to address any ethical concerns that may arise.

Additionally, be transparent about the capabilities and limitations of your chatbot. Clearly communicate the purpose and scope of the chatbot to users to manage their expectations. Avoid making false claims or overpromising results.

Regularly review and update your chatbot's policies, terms of service, and privacy statements to reflect any changes in legal requirements or ethical considerations. Stay informed about emerging trends, best practices, and industry guidelines related to chatbot compliance and security to ensure ongoing adherence to standards.

By prioritizing compliance with legal and privacy considerations, securing user information, implementing safeguards against malicious activities, and maintaining ethical standards in chatbot interactions, you can build trust with users and mitigate risks associated with privacy breaches, legal issues, and unethical practices.

Chapter 6. Chatbot Success Stories

A. Case studies of businesses that have successfully monetized chatbots

B. Lessons learned and key takeaways from their experiences

C. Insights into their strategies and implementation approaches

A. Case Studies of Businesses that have Successfully Monetized Chatbots

Starbucks: Starbucks launched a chatbot on the Facebook Messenger platform called "My Starbucks Barista." Customers can place orders and make payments through the chatbot, simplifying the ordering process. The chatbot's success lies in its seamless integration with the Starbucks mobile app, loyalty program, and payment systems, providing a convenient and personalized experience for users.

Sephora: Sephora implemented a chatbot on Kik, a messaging app popular among younger audiences. The chatbot offers makeup tips, product recommendations, and allows users to try on virtual makeup. Sephora's chatbot leverages interactive and engaging features, helping users discover products and make informed purchasing decisions. The chatbot also collects user data to personalize recommendations, further enhancing the user experience.

Domino's Pizza: Domino's Pizza introduced a chatbot called "Dom" on various messaging platforms, including Facebook Messenger, Slack, and Amazon Alexa. Users can place pizza orders, track deliveries, and access personalized offers through the chatbot. Dom's success lies in its simplicity and focus on streamlining the ordering process, providing convenience and speed to customers.

B. Lessons Learned and Key Takeaways from their Experiences

Seamless Integration: Successful chatbots seamlessly integrate with existing systems, such as mobile apps, payment gateways, and loyalty programs. This integration enhances the user experience and simplifies processes, leading to higher user adoption and engagement.

Personalization and Recommendations: Chatbots that leverage user data to provide personalized recommendations and offers can significantly enhance the user experience. By analyzing user preferences and behavior, chatbots can deliver tailored suggestions, increasing customer satisfaction and driving sales.

Simplicity and Convenience: Chatbots that prioritize simplicity and convenience resonate well with users. They streamline processes, reduce friction, and make tasks easier to accomplish. By focusing on user needs and providing quick solutions, chatbots can deliver a positive user experience.

C. Insights into their Strategies and Implementation Approaches

User-Centric Approach: Successful chatbots prioritize the needs and preferences of their target audience. They understand their users' pain points and design chatbot interactions and features to address those pain points effectively.

Multichannel Availability: Successful chatbots are available on multiple messaging platforms, catering to a wider user base. This approach ensures accessibility and meets users on their preferred platforms, increasing engagement and usage.

Continuous Improvement: The success of chatbots is not static but evolves over time. Successful implementations involve continuous monitoring, analysis, and improvement based on user feedback and data insights. Iterative enhancements and updates ensure that chatbots remain relevant and valuable to users.

By studying these successful chatbot implementations and understanding the key factors that contributed to their success, businesses can gain insights and inspiration for their own chatbot strategies. It is essential to tailor these strategies to their specific industry, target audience, and business goals to maximize their chatbot's potential for success.

Chapter 7. Future Trends and Opportunities

A. Emerging technologies and innovations in the chatbot space

B. Predictions for the future of chatbot monetization

C. Opportunities for business growth and expansion through chatbots

A. Emerging Technologies and Innovations in the Chatbot Space

Natural Language Processing (NLP) Advancements: NLP technology continues to evolve, enabling chatbots to better understand and respond to user queries with increased accuracy and context. Improved NLP algorithms and techniques will lead to more conversational and human-like interactions between chatbots and users.

Voice-Activated Chatbots: With the rise of smart speakers and voice assistants, voice-activated chatbots will become more prevalent. Chatbots will be integrated with voice platforms, allowing users to interact with them through spoken commands, further enhancing convenience and accessibility.

Artificial Intelligence (AI) Enhancements: AI advancements will enable chatbots to learn from user interactions, adapt to user preferences, and provide more personalized and tailored experiences. Machine learning algorithms and predictive analytics will help chatbots anticipate user needs and deliver proactive recommendations.

B. Predictions for the Future of Chatbot Monetization

Enhanced E-commerce Integration: Chatbots will continue to play a significant role in e-commerce, with improved integration capabilities. Chatbots will facilitate seamless product discovery, personalized recommendations, and simplified checkout processes, driving increased conversion rates and revenue generation.

Premium Chatbot Services: As chatbots become more sophisticated, businesses may offer premium chatbot services for advanced features or specialized expertise. Users may be willing to pay for exclusive access to premium chatbots that provide enhanced functionality, personalized assistance, or industry-specific knowledge.

Chatbot-as-a-Service (CaaS): With the growing demand for chatbot solutions, the CaaS model will gain traction. Businesses can offer scalable and customizable chatbot platforms, allowing other companies to build and deploy their own chatbot applications without extensive development resources.

C. Opportunities for Business Growth and Expansion through Chatbots

Improved Customer Service: Chatbots present opportunities for businesses to enhance their customer service capabilities. By providing instant and accurate responses to customer inquiries, chatbots can improve response times, reduce customer wait times, and enhance overall customer satisfaction.

Personalized Marketing and Sales: Chatbots can collect and analyze user data, enabling businesses to deliver personalized marketing messages and tailored product recommendations. By leveraging user preferences and behaviors, chatbots can drive targeted marketing campaigns and increase conversion rates.

Streamlined Operations and Cost Reduction: Chatbots can automate repetitive tasks, such as answering FAQs, processing orders, and providing basic support. This automation can streamline operations, reduce manual effort, and lower costs for businesses, allowing them to allocate resources more efficiently.

Expansion into New Channels: Chatbots can be deployed on various messaging platforms, social media platforms, websites, and mobile apps. Businesses can leverage these channels to reach new audiences, expand their market reach, and engage customers on platforms where they spend their time.

By embracing emerging technologies, capitalizing on chatbot monetization opportunities, and leveraging chatbots for improved customer service, personalized marketing, streamlined operations, and expansion into new channels, businesses can position themselves for growth and success in the future. It is important for businesses to stay updated on the latest trends and continuously innovate their chatbot strategies to stay competitive in the evolving landscape.

Conclusion

A. Recap of key concepts and strategies discussed

B. Final words of encouragement and inspiration

C. Call to action to start monetizing chatbots and make money

A. Recap of Key Concepts and Strategies Discussed

We have explored various important concepts and strategies related to monetizing chatbots:

Understanding legal and privacy considerations for chatbots, complying with data protection regulations, and securing user information.

Implementing safeguards against malicious activities and fraud, ensuring the security and trustworthiness of chatbot interactions.

Maintaining ethical standards in chatbot interactions to build trust and avoid deceptive practices.

Examining success stories of businesses that successfully monetized chatbots and learning from their experiences and strategies.

Exploring emerging technologies and innovations in the chatbot space, such as advancements in natural language processing, voice-activated chatbots, and AI enhancements.

Predicting future trends in chatbot monetization, including enhanced e-commerce integration, premium chatbot services, and the Chatbot-as-a-Service model.

Identifying opportunities for business growth and expansion through chatbots, including improved customer service, personalized marketing and sales, streamlined operations, and expansion into new channels.

B. Final Words of Encouragement and Inspiration

Monetizing chatbots presents a world of opportunities for businesses to enhance customer experiences, streamline operations, and drive revenue growth. By leveraging the concepts, strategies, and future trends discussed, you can position your business for success in the evolving landscape of chatbot monetization.

Remember that innovation and adaptation are crucial in this fast-paced field. Stay curious, embrace emerging technologies, and continuously iterate your chatbot strategies to meet evolving user expectations and market demands.

C. Call to Action to Start Monetizing Chatbots and Make Money

Now is the time to act and capitalize on the potential of chatbot monetization. Analyze your business needs, identify opportunities for chatbot implementation, and start strategizing your approach. Consider partnering with experts in chatbot development and deployment to ensure a smooth and successful implementation.

With the right planning, execution, and ongoing optimization, you can create chatbots that enhance customer experiences, drive revenue, and position your business at the forefront of innovation.

Embrace the power of chatbots, seize the opportunities before you, and embark on your journey to monetize chatbots and make a positive impact on your business.

Appendix

A. Resources for chatbot development platforms and tools

B. Glossary of key terms and acronyms

C. Frequently asked questions (FAQs) about chatbot monetization

A. Resources for Chatbot Development Platforms and Tools

Dialogflow by Google: A powerful and user-friendly platform for building AI-powered chatbots and virtual agents, offering natural language understanding and integration with various messaging platforms.

IBM Watson Assistant: A comprehensive chatbot development platform that leverages AI and natural language processing to build chatbots capable of interacting with users across multiple channels.

Microsoft Azure Bot Service: A cloud-based platform for building, deploying, and managing intelligent chatbots, providing tools and services for natural language understanding and conversation management.

Botpress: An open-source chatbot development framework that offers a visual interface, advanced NLP capabilities, and integration options with popular messaging platforms.

B. Glossary of Key Terms and Acronyms

NLP: Natural Language Processing - A field of AI that focuses on the interaction between computers and human language, enabling chatbots to understand and interpret human language.

AI: Artificial Intelligence - The simulation of human intelligence in machines, allowing them to perform tasks that typically require human intelligence, such as natural language understanding and decision-making.

CaaS: Chatbot-as-a-Service - A model in which businesses provide chatbot platforms as a service, allowing other companies to build and deploy their own chatbot applications without extensive development resources.

FAQ: Frequently Asked Questions - A compilation of common questions and their corresponding answers, often used to provide quick and standardized information to users.

C. Frequently Asked Questions (FAQs) about Chatbot Monetization

Q1: How can I monetize my chatbot?

A: There are several ways to monetize chatbots, including integrating e-commerce functionality, offering premium services, partnering with other businesses for sponsored content or advertising, and providing chatbot development services to clients.

Q2: Are there any legal considerations for monetizing chatbots?

A: Yes, it is essential to comply with data protection regulations, ensure user privacy, and have clear terms of service and privacy policies. Consult legal experts to ensure your chatbot complies with relevant laws and regulations.

Q3: How can chatbots improve customer service and support?

A: Chatbots can provide instant responses, 24/7 availability, and personalized assistance to customers, reducing response times and enhancing overall customer satisfaction.

Q4: What are the future trends in chatbot monetization?

A: Future trends include enhanced e-commerce integration, premium chatbot services, voice-activated chatbots, and the Chatbot-as-a-Service model.

Q5: How can I measure the success of my monetized chatbot?

A: Key metrics to track include user engagement, conversion rates, revenue generated, customer satisfaction ratings, and feedback and reviews from users.

Please note that these answers are general and may vary depending on your specific use case and industry. It is recommended to conduct further research and consult with professionals to tailor your chatbot monetization strategy to your unique circumstances.